W9-CPM-811

GRAPHIC HISTORY

THE VOYAGE OF THE Mayflower

by Allison Lassieur
illustrated by Peter McDonnell

Consultant:
Walter W. Woodward
Assistant Professor of History
University of Connecticut, Hartford

Capstone
press

Mankato, Minnesota

Graphic Library is published by Capstone Press,
151 Good Counsel Drive, P.O. Box 669, Mankato, Minnesota 56002.
www.capstonepress.com

1 2 3 4 5 6 10 09 08 07 06 05

Library of Congress Cataloging-in-Publication Data
Lassieur, Allison.
The voyage of the Mayflower / by Allison Lassieur; illustrated by Peter McDonnell.
    p. cm.—(Graphic library. Graphic history)
    Summary: "In graphic novel format, tells the story of the colonists who traveled to North
America in 1620 on the Mayflower, their reasons for coming, and how they started Plymouth
Colony"—Provided by publisher.
    Includes bibliographical references and index.
    ISBN 0-7368-4371-X (hardcover)
    1. Mayflower (Ship)—Juvenile literature. 2. Pilgrims (New Plymouth Colony)—Juvenile
literature. 3. Massachusetts—History—New Plymouth, 1620–1691—Juvenile literature.
I. McDonnell, Peter, ill. II. Title. III. Series.
F68.L37 2006
974.4'8202—dc22   2005008109

Art and Editorial Direction
Jason Knudson and Blake A. Hoena

Designer
Jason Knudson

Editor
Rebecca Glaser

Editor's note: Direct quotations from primary sources are indicated by a yellow background.

Direct quotations appear on the following pages:
Page 7 (both), from *Of Plymouth Plantation* by William Bradford (New York: Alfred Knopf,
    1952.)
Page 11, letter from John Robinson to congregation, printed in *Of Plymouth Plantation* by
    William Bradford (New York: Alfred Knopf, 1952.)
Page 13, letter from Robert Cushman, printed in *Of Plymouth Plantation* by William Bradford
    (New York: Alfred Knopf, 1952.)
Page 23, from *Of Plymouth Plantation* by William Bradford (New York: Alfred Knopf, 1952.)

Table of Contents

CHAPTER 1

Plans for a New Life

England had one official church in the early 1600s. If you didn't belong to the Church of England, you were breaking the law. Some groups were willing to worship secretly and risk arrest to practice their own beliefs. One of these groups was the Separatists. They wanted to follow God's word simply, without the extra rules set by the Church of England.

By order of the king, you're under arrest! This church is illegal.

By 1609, 125 members of one Separatist group had fled to Leiden, Holland. Pastor John Robinson led the congregation.

We thank God that we can worship freely here.

The work here in Holland is very hard.

We could get better jobs if we had been born here.

After about 12 years, the Separatists' lives in Leiden had not improved.

Our family stays poor, no matter how hard we work.

Our children now speak more Dutch than English.

CHAPTER 2

A Troubled Start

The Separatists could not pay for the trip on their own. In London, John Carver and another Separatist, Robert Cushman, made a deal with businessman Thomas Weston.

Back in Holland, Separatist families sold some of their belongings to pay for the trip.

Mr. Cushman, I'll lend you some money for your trip. Your group must come up with the rest.

How much can I get for this ring?

Sorry, it's not worth much.

Thank you, Mr. Weston. We'll pay you back in seven years, with lumber and furs from Virginia.

Mother, I could sell my doll.

CHAPTER 3

The Mayflower Voyage

After several weeks' delay, the *Mayflower* set sail in good weather on September 6, 1620. Of the 102 passengers, fewer than half were Separatists. The others had come along for different reasons.

Watch where you're going!

Captain Christopher Jones and his crew had been hired to sail the ship. They did not plan to settle in Virginia.

17

Everyone was eager to leave the ship, but there was a problem. The Separatists had a charter giving them permission to settle in Virginia, not Massachusetts. The Strangers wanted to go their own way.

The charter doesn't apply here. No one can govern us.

If the Strangers leave us, we'll never survive.

When we go ashore, we'll use our own liberty.

And we'll never be able to pay our debt.

We must find a way to keep the group together.

The Separatist leaders drew up an agreement, later known as the Mayflower Compact. It said that the Separatists and Strangers would join together for the government of the colony. All but a few servants signed it.

More about the Mayflower

- The people on the *Mayflower* did not call themselves pilgrims. William Bradford first gave that name to the colonists in his book *Of Plymouth Plantation*. Bradford wrote this account during his lifetime, but it was not published until the 1800s.

- The *Mayflower* was built as a cargo ship. Before the ship transported people, it was used to carry wine and furs.

- The original *Mayflower* no longer exists. It is thought that parts of it were later used to build the roof of a barn in Buckinghamshire, England.

- William Mullins, a shoe and boot salesman, brought more than 250 shoes and 13 pairs of boots on the *Mayflower*. He hoped to sell them to the colonists.

- A young passenger named Francis Billington almost set the *Mayflower* on fire. He shot a musket inside a cabin near an open barrel of gunpowder.

During the voyage, Elizabeth Hopkins gave birth to a baby boy. She named him Oceanus because he was born on the ocean.

Many of the *Mayflower's* passengers got terribly seasick.

Only one person died while the *Mayflower* was at sea. He was a sailor who died from disease.

Passengers on the *Mayflower:*
        50 men
        19 women
        14 teenagers
        19 children

The average age of the men on the *Mayflower* was 34.

Glossary

cargo (KAR-goh)—freight that is carried by a ship

charter (CHAR-tur)—a document that gives a group the right to create a colony on a certain area of land and provides for a government

contract (KAHN-trakt)—a written agreement between two or more people or groups

elder (ELL-dur)—a leader of a religious group who is not a pastor or priest

invincible (in-VIN-suh-buhl)—incapable of being defeated

New World (NEW WURLD)—a term used by early colonists to refer to North America

plague (PLAYG)—a serious disease that spreads quickly to many people and often causes death

sabotage (SA-buh-tahzh)—to purposely destroy property to stop an activity

Internet Sites

FactHound offers a safe, fun way to find Internet sites related to this book. All of the sites on FactHound have been researched by our staff.

Here's how:

1. *Visit www.facthound.com*
2. Type in this special code **073684371X** for age-appropriate sites. Or enter a search word related to this book for a more general search.
3. Click on the **Fetch It** button.

FactHound will fetch the best sites for you!

Read More

Apel, Melanie Ann. *The Pilgrims.* Daily Life. San Diego: KidHaven Press, 2003.

Brooks, Phillip. *The Mayflower Compact.* We the People. Minneapolis: Compass Point Books, 2005.

Dell, Pamela. *The Plymouth Colony.* Let Freedom Ring. Mankato, Minn.: Capstone Press, 2004.

Hirschfelder, Arlene B. *Squanto: 1585?–1622.* American Indian Biographes. Mankato, Minn.: Blue Earth Books, 2004.

Plimoth Plantation. *Mayflower 1620: A New Look at a Pilgrim Voyage.* Washington, D.C.: National Geographic, 2003.

Bibiliography

Bradford, William. *Of Plymouth Plantation.* New York: Alfred Knopf, 1952.

Caffrey, Kate. *The Mayflower.* New York: Stein and Day, 1974.

Deetz, James, and Patricia Scott Deetz. *The Times of Their Lives: Life, Love, and Death in Plymouth Colony.* New York: W.H. Freeman, 2000.

Dillon, Francis. *The Pilgrims.* Garden City, N. Y.: Doubleday, 1975.

Mourt, G. *Mourt's Relation: A Journal of the Pilgrims at Plymouth.* New York: Corinth Books, 1963.

Index